D0873628

CLOSING TIME

CLOSING

TIME

NORMAN O. BROWN

VINTAGE BOOKS

A Division of Random House   New York

FIRST VINTAGE BOOKS EDITION, September 1974

Copyright © 1973 by Norton R. Potter, as Trustee

Library of Congress Cataloging in Publication Data

Brown, Norman Oliver, 1913–
    Closing time.
    Bibliography: p.
    1. Joyce, James, 1882–1941. Finnegans wake.
2. Vico, Giovanni Battista, 1668–1744. L'Autobio-
grafia.   3. Vico, Giovanni Battista, 1668–1744.
Principi di una scienza nuova. I. Title.
[PR6019.09F565 1974]   823'.9'12   74–4226
ISBN 0–394–71161–0

*Grateful acknowledgment is made for permission
to reprint the following material:*

Excerpts from *The New Science of Giambattista Vico:*
Revised Translation of the Third Edition (1744) by
Thomas Goddard Bergin and Max Harold Fisch. Copyright
© 1968 by Cornell University, Copyright © 1961 by
Thomas Goddard Bergin and Max Harold Fisch,
Copyright 1948 by Cornell University. Excerpts from
The Autobiography of Giambattista Vico, translated by
Max Harold Fisch and Thomas Goddard Bergin. Copyright
1944 by Cornell University. Used by permission of Cornell
University Press.

"To the Reader" from *The Jacob's Ladder* by Denise
Levertov. Copyright © 1961 by Denise Levertov Goodman.
Reprinted by permission of New Directions Publishing
Corporation and Jonathan Cape Ltd.

Excerpts and drawing from *Finnegans Wake* by James
Joyce. Copyright 1939 by James Joyce, © 1967 by George
Joyce and Lucia Joyce. All rights reserved. Reprinted by
permission of The Viking Press, Inc. and The Society
of Authors as the literary representative of the Estate of
James Joyce.

BIBLIOGRAPHY

T. G. Bergin and M. H. Fisch
The New Science of Giambattista Vico (Ithaca, New York, 1968)
Cited by paragraph number

M. H. Fisch and T. G. Bergin
The Autobiography of Giambattista Vico (Ithaca, New York, 1963)

I. Berlin
"The Philosophical Ideas of Giambattista Vico,"
Art and Ideas in Eighteenth-Century Italy (Rome, 1960),
pages 156–244

J. Joyce
Finnegans Wake (New York, 1966)

N. O. Brown
Love's Body (New York, 1966)

All quotations from either Vico or Joyce are printed in italics.

PREFACE

Time, gentlemen, please?
The question is addressed to Giambattista Vico and
James Joyce.
Vico, *New Science*; with Joyce, *Finnegans Wake*.
"Two books get on top of each other and become
sexual."
Two books on top of each other—
John Cage told me that this is geometrically im-
possible.
But let us try it.

> *The book of Doublends Jined.*   FW, 20

At least we can try to stuff *Finnegans Wake* into
Vico's *New Science*.

> *One world burrowing on another.*   FW, 275

To make a farce.

> *What a mnice old mness it all mnakes!*   FW, 19

Confusion, source of renewal, says Ezra Pound.
Or as James Joyce puts it in *Finnegans Wake*:

> *First mull a mugfull of mud, son.*   FW, 286

> *As rational metaphysics teaches that man be-*
> *comes all things by understanding them* (HOMO IN-
> TELLIGENDO FIT OMNIA), *this imaginative metaphysics*
> *shows that man becomes all things by not under-*
> *standing them* (HOMO NON INTELLIGENDO FIT OMNIA).   NS, 405

CONTENTS

CLOSING TIME

I. The Delineaments of Giants

Vico a giant
> let us praise and magnify his name
>> *Finn, again!*   FW, 628
> as it was in the beginning
> there were giants on the earth in those days

Vico is *ricorso*

Vico is a giant, like HCE
the mystery of size: the great man, how small he is!
>> *How small it's all!*   FW, 627

Here Comes Everybody
Haveth Childers Everywhere
is also Humphrey Chimpden Earwicker

Vico is also a very foolish fond old man

No better than a fool as a father:

the bad character which one of his sons showed from childhood. When he had grown up, far from applying himself to studies and sober habits, he became addicted to a soft and lazy life, and as time went on to all sorts of vices, so that he became the dishonor of the entire family. No measure was overlooked by the good father to bring his son back from his erring ways and set him again on the right path. Repeated and affectionate admonishments, authoritative warnings from men of wisdom and reputation, all proved useless efforts to reform the errant youth. Things came to such a pass indeed that the sorrowing father found himself against his will in the hard necessity of calling in the police to have his son imprisoned. But at the last minute, when he heard the police coming up the stairs of his house and bethought himself of their errand, he was carried away by paternal love, ran to his unhappy son and said to him, trembling: "Save yourself, my son." But this act of fatherly tenderness did not prevent justice from taking its inevitable course; for the boy was taken to prison and spent a long time there before he gave clear signs of having really mended his ways.

Autob. 203

A fool or worse in politics:

He eked out his low income by accepting commissions from the rich and the great to write Latin inscriptions, official obituaries and laudatory biographies of important persons. The best known of these are his life of Antonio Caraffa, a Neapolitan soldier who crushed a Hungarian rebellion in the service of the Emperor, and his history of the Macchia conspiracy. This last was a plot at the turn of the century to replace Spanish by Austrian rule in Naples. It was uncovered, and in 1701 the ringleaders were duly executed by the Spaniards. In 1702 Vico published an account of the conspiracy, denouncing the participants as criminals and traitors. Five years later the Austrians occupied Naples and held it for the next twenty-seven years. In 1708 Vico issued a memorial volume which made no reference to the earlier work and celebrated the two chief conspirators as patriots and martyrs. In 1734 Naples was reconquered by Charles de Bourbon. He was duly offered humble congratulations by Vico at the head of a delegation sent by the University of Naples, and graciously appointed Vico historiographer royal.

Berlin, 158

An academic failure:

    The concourse for Capasso's chair and others vacated in the meantime was finally announced in January, 1723. Vico promptly entered his name. He delivered his concourse lecture on a fragment of the DIGEST *on April 10, blissfully unaware that the commission of judges was already divided into two factions, both committed to other candidates. Of the twenty-nine votes, fifteen were cast for one of these and fourteen for the other. The winner, Domenico Gentile, a notorious seducer of servant girls (he later committed suicide over one of them) was so incapable of writing a book of any sort that his one attempt was withdrawn from the press after being exposed as a plagiarism.*

Autob. 10

Shem the Pen no match for Shaun the Post.

A providential failure, which freed him to write the New Science:

All the other poor works of my mind I owe to myself because they were devised for my own ends, with a view to winning an honorable station in my native city; but since our university has considered me unworthy of one, I assuredly owe this work entirely to it, for its unwillingness to have me occupied in expounding paragraphs from the PANDECTS *has left me the leisure to compose it. Forever praised be Providence, which, when the weak sight of mortals sees in it nothing but stern justice, then most of all is at work on a crowning mercy! For by this work I feel myself clothed upon with a new man; I no longer wince at the things that once goaded me to bewail my hard lot and to denounce the corruption of letters that has caused that lot; for this corruption and this lot have strengthened me and enabled me to perfect this work. Moreover (if it be not true, I like to think it is) this work has filled me with a certain heroic spirit, so that I am no longer troubled by any fear of death, nor have I any mind to speak of rivals.*

Autob.
14–15

Vico's life, as in *Finnegans Wake*.

First we fall:

> The great fall of the offwall entailed at such
> short notice the pftjschute of Finnegan

FW, 3

> Giambattista Vico was born in Naples in the
> year 1670 of upright parents who left a good name
> after them. His father was of a cheerful disposition,
> his mother of a quite melancholy temper; both con-
> tributed to the character of their child. He was a boy
> of high spirits and impatient of rest; but at the age
> of seven he fell head first from the top of a ladder
> to the floor below, and remained a good five hours
> without motion or consciousness. The right side of
> the cranium was fractured, but the skin was not
> broken. The fracture gave rise to a large tumor, and
> the child suffered much loss of blood from the many
> deep lancings. The surgeon, indeed, observing the
> broken cranium and considering the long period of
> unconsciousness, predicted that he would either die
> of it or grow up an idiot. However by God's grace
> neither part of his prediction came true, but as a
> result of this mischance he grew up with a melan-
> choly and irritable temperament such as belongs to
> men of ingenuity and depth, who, thanks to the one,
> are quick as lightning in perception, and thanks to
> the other, take no pleasure in verbal cleverness or
> falsehood.

Autob. 111

Then we feud:

Vico was choleric to a fault. Though he guarded himself from it as best he could in his writing, he publicly confessed his failing. He would inveigh too violently against the errors of thought or scholarship or against the misconduct of those men of letters who were his rivals, which as a charitable Christian or a true philosopher he should rather have over-looked or pitied. But if he was bitter toward those who belittled him and his works, he was correspond-ingly grateful to those who formed a just opinion of both; and the latter were always the best and the most learned men of the city. Among the caitiff semi-learned or pseudo-learned, the more shameless called him a fool, or in somewhat more courteous terms they said that he was obscure or eccentric and had odd ideas. He however blessed all these adversi-ties as so many occasions for withdrawing to his desk, as to his high impregnable citadel, to meditate and to write further works which he was wont to call "so many noble acts of vengeance against his detrac-tors." These finally led him to the discovery of his NEW SCIENCE.

Autob.
199–200

A bad wake:

It was the custom for the professors of the Royal University to accompany to the sepulcher the remains of their departed colleagues; a praiseworthy custom which has survived the lapse of so many others. When the hour for Vico's funeral rites had been set, almost all the professors were eager to pay this last tribute to their deceased colleague and came to his house to accompany the remains. The Confraternity of Santa Sophia, of which Vico had been a member, were to carry the coffin as they regularly did for their deceased members. When the Confraternity arrived at his house, they began to murmur that they would not allow the professors of the University to bear the pall. The professors on the other hand contended they had the right to that honor, and adduced many precedents. Meanwhile the corpse was carried down into the courtyard of the house and laid on the bier, which bore the arms of the Royal University. Hereupon there began a great uproar between the members of the Confraternity and the professors of the University, neither side being willing to yield to the other, and both showing in the presence of the dead how far human weakness and pride can go. As no amicable understanding could be reached, the Confraternity, with small regard for human decency, decided to take their leave, abandoning the corpse where it lay. The professors alone were unable to carry out the funeral rites, and the corpse had to be carried back into its old dwelling.

Lovesoftfun at Finnegan's Wake.   FW, 607

   A good clap, a fore marriage, a bad wake, tell
hell's well.   FW, 117
   Forever praised be Providence.   Autob. 15

II. The New Science of History

A New Science—
like Bacon's *Novum Organum*
a Copernican revolution
to turn us around.

> (In praise of the Bergin and Fisch translation
> extraordinary professors
> they love Vico more than they love themselves
> the texture of the original
> Vico belongs to us
> Italians found Michelet's translation more intelligible than the original
> and Salvemini had said "English is an honest language; there will be nothing left of Vico.")

The New Science, of man
                              (anthropology
man as maker
              (*homo faber*
science is of making
scire est per causas scire
knowledge is knowledge of causes
to know is to know how to make it
                                    (to have made it
v. Descartes' clear and distinct ideas:
    In geometry we demonstrate because we create.
    The rule and criterion of truth is to have made it.   Autob. 38

The true (*verum*) and the made (*factum*) are
convertible   Berlin, 165
verification is fabrication
fact is fabrication
homo faber
man the forger; at his forge
forging the uncreated conscience of his race.

To know is to have made it
only God can know the physical world
but *"the world of civil society has certainly been
made by men, and its principles are therefore to be
found within the modifications of our own human
mind."*

NS, 331

Compare Hobbes:

Of arts, some are demonstrable, others in-
demonstrable; and demonstrable are those the construction of the subject whereof is in the power of
the artist himself, who, in his demonstration, does no
more but deduce the consequences of his own oper-
ation. The reason whereof is this, that the science of
every subject is derived from a precognition of the
causes, generation, and construction of the same; and
consequently where the causes are known, there is
place for demonstration, but not where the causes
are to seek for. Geometry therefore is demonstrable,
for the lines and figures from which we reason are
drawn and described by ourselves; *and civil philosophy is demonstrable, because we make the common-
wealth ourselves.* But because of natural bodies we
know not the construction, but seek it from the
effects, there lies no demonstration of what the
causes be we seek for, but only of what they may be.

Autob.
40–41

History cannot be more certain than when he
who creates the things also narrates them.　　NS, 349
In history man makes himself

(Gordon Childe and the
Marxists

We shall show clearly and distinctly how the
founders of gentile humanity by means of their nat-
ural theology (or metaphysics) imagined the gods;
how by means of their logic they invented languages;
by morals, created heroes; by economics, founded
families, and by politics, cities; by their physics, es-
tablished the beginnings of things as all divine; by
the particular physics of man, in a certain sense
created themselves.　　NS, 367

Man makes himself, even his own body.   *Love's Body,*
The human body a historical variable   127
                                        (Freud
history begins with bestial giants
                                        (as in *Finnegans Wake*
    The brontoichthyan form   FW, 7
    In the name of Anem this carl on the kopje in
pelted thongs a parth a lone who the joebiggar be
he? Forshapen his pigmaid hoagshead, shroonk his
plodsfoot. He hath locktoes, this shortshins, and,
Obeold that's pectoral, his mammamuscles most
mousterious.   FW, 15

The making of man is education
educing humanity
    Heroic education began to bring forth in a cer-
tain way the form of the human soul which had
been completely submerged in the huge bodies of
the giants, and began likewise to bring forth the
form of the human body itself in its just dimensions
from the disproportionate giant bodies.   NS, 520

As for the other part of household discipline, the education of bodies, the fathers with their frightful religions, their cyclopean authority, and their sacred ablutions began to educe, or bring forth, from the giant bodies of their sons the proper human form.

NS, 524

As with Freud, it is primarily a matter of toilet training:

Mothers, like beasts, must merely have nursed their babies, let them wallow naked in their own filth. And these children, who had to wallow in their own filth, whose nitrous salts richly fertilized the fields, and who had to exert themselves to penetrate the great forest, would flex and contract their muscles in these exertions, and thus absorb nitrous salts into their bodies in greater abundance. They would be quite without that fear of gods, fathers, and teachers which chills and benumbs even the most exuberant in childhood. They must therefore have grown up robust, vigorous, excessively big in brawn and bone, to the point of becoming giants.

NS, 369

Therefore:

Civilization began with water. It was by becoming imbued with this cleanliness of body and this fear of gods and of fathers that the giants diminished to our normal stature. It was perhaps for this reason that from POLITEIA, which in Greek means civil government, was derived the Latin POLITUS, meaning clean or neat.

NS, 371

The polis is polished
civilization is polite
         is policed.

The entire original human race was divided into two species: the one of giants, the other men of normal stature; the former gentiles, the latter Hebrews.

NS, 172

The Hebrews, on account of their cleanly upbringing and their fear of God and of their fathers, continued to be of the proper stature in which God had created Adam and Noah procreated his three sons; and it was perhaps in abomination of giantism that the Hebrews had so many ceremonial rules pertaining to bodily cleanliness.

NS, 371

* * * * *

A New Science: the genetic method
scire est per causas scire
to know is to know how it comes into being
coming-into-being and passing-away
Aristotle's genesis; the Bible's Genesis
in the beginning
ab ovo:
    eggburst, eggblend, eggburial and
hatch-as-hatch can.

FW, 614

History is not historicism but origins
*The Origin of the Family, Private Property, and the
State.*   Engels
Principles are first beginnings
>   *Doctrines must take their beginning from that
of the matters of which they treat.*   NS, 314

primaque ab origine mundi
principles take us back to the primordial
principles take us back to primitives
The New Science:

>   *It must begin where its subject matter began, as
we said in the Axioms. We must therefore go back
with the philologians and fetch it from the stones of
Deucalion and Pyrrha, from the rocks of Amphion,
from the men who sprang from the furrows of Cad-
mus, or the hard oaks of Vergil. With the philosophers we must fetch it from the frogs of Epicurus,
from the cicadas of Hobbes, from the simpletons of
Grotius; from the men cast into this world without
care or aid of God, of whom Pufendorf speaks, as
gross and wild as the giants called "Big Feet," who
are said to be found near the Strait of Magellan;
which is as much as to say from the cyclopes of
Homer, in whom Plato recognizes the first fathers
in the state of the families.*   NS, 338

Genesis is Natura
the nature of nations is their *nascimento*   NS, 147–48
           the way they were born
culture is nature
the nations have a natural law which is their nature   NS, 311
           the way they were born
the Vico Rd is the Nascimiento Rd   FW, 452
           (below Big Sur
the way they were born
the birth trauma
       (Otto Rank
determines their character
the nature of nations is their nativity
the New Science is astrology
casting the horoscope of nations
the hour of their birth is the hour of their death
under what sign were they born
the New Science is a science of signs and wonders
in Vico's terms, augury; observing the auspices   NS, 9
the New Science a return to divination   NS, 342
       contemplation
    In their science of augury the Romans used the
verb CONTEMPLARI *for observing the parts of the sky*
when the auspices were taken. These regions, marked
out by augurs with their wands, were called temples
of the sky.   NS, 391

Principles; primordial; primeval; archetypal—
the royal stamp, the original principle
the ruling principle is in the beginning
                    EN APXHI
primordial, primeval: German *Ur*—
origin as *Ur-sprung*, primeval leap
causality as *Ur-sache*, primeval thing
Ur-zeit, primeval time; that time before time began
                         in illo tempore
                                   (Eliade

Ur-kunde as the form of knowing:
      kenning, the Akashic archives
Ur; Ur of the Chaldees.

Back to the first beginnings
Finnagain Beginnagain
      by a commodius vicus of recirculation
back to Howth Castle and Environs.   FW, 3

          *   *   *   *   *

A New Science: the cyclical view of history—

The pattern of *Finnegans Wake* is loosely derived from the Italian philosopher Giovanni Battista Vico (1668–1744), who wrote an important book called *La Scienza Nuova*, in which he presented history not as a straight line but as a circular process of recurrences.

Burgess,
Shorter
FW, xii

The cyclical view of history
a cycle of world ages
as in the mystical tradition, the occult tradition
The New Science is The Secret Doctrine
Vico is an Orphic Voice

H. P. Blavatsky

E. Sewell

      Platonist, he says:

Vico felt himself dissatisfied with the metaphysic of Aristotle as an aid to the understanding of moral philosophy, and found himself instructed by that of Plato. For the metaphysics of Aristotle leads to a physical principle, which is matter, from which the particular forms are drawn; and indeed makes God a potter who works at things outside himself. But the metaphysics of Plato leads to a metaphysical principle, which is the eternal idea, drawing out and creating matter from itself, like a seminal spirit that forms its own egg.

Autob. 121

Vico says he took it from the Egyptians
                    (Helen in Egypt
                    (H.D. studying the mysteries

Thus from the Egyptians, who twitted the Greeks for being always children and knowing nothing of antiquity, he takes and puts to use two great fragments of antiquity. One of these is their division of all preceding times into three ages: (1) the age of the gods, in which the gentiles believed they lived under divine governments, and every thing was commanded them by auspices and oracles, which are the oldest institutions in profane history; (2) the age of heroes, in which they reigned everywhere in aristocratic commonwealths, on account of a certain superiority of nature which they held themselves to have over the plebeians; (3) the age of men, in which all men recognized themselves as equal in human nature, and therefore there were established first the popular commonwealths and then the monarchies, both of which are forms of human government. The other thing he took from the Egyptians is their reduction of the languages spoken before their time to three types, coeval respectively with the three ages. First the divine, a dumb language of hieroglyphics or sacred characters. Second, the symbolic, consisting of metaphors as the heroic language did. Third, the epistolographic or vulgar, consisting of expressions agreed upon for the everyday uses of life.

Autob. 169

NS, 31

First the age of the gods, then the age of heroes, then the age of men.
It is a cycle of decline; as in Plato's *Republic*.

Men first feel necessity, then look for utility, next attend to comfort, still later amuse themselves with pleasure, thence grow dissolute in luxury, and finally go mad and waste their substance.   NS, 241

That's where it's at: decline.

The Decline of the West   O. Spengler

A graffito (hieroglyph) from May 1968 in Paris: "America is the only nation in history to go from barbarism to decadence with no civilization in between."

The hand is the hand of a Paris student, but the voice is the voice of Vico.

First the age of the gods, then the age of heroes, then the age of men.

The origin is sacred; the decline is secularization, process is profanation:

I sometimes think I see that civilizations originate in the disclosure of some mystery, some secret; and expand with the progressive publication of their secret; and end in exhaustion when there is no longer any secret, when the mystery has been divulged, that is to say profaned. The whole story is illustrated in the difference between ideogram and alphabet. The alphabet is indeed a democratic triumph; and the enigmatic ideogram, as Ezra Pound has taught us, is a piece of mystery, a piece of poetry, not yet profaned. And so there comes a time—I believe we are in such a time—when civilization has to be renewed by the discovery of new mysteries, by the undemocratic but sovereign power of the imagination, by the undemocratic power which makes poets the unacknowledged legislators of mankind, the power which makes all things new.

N. O. Brown
"Apocalypse"
Harper's
May 1961

The origin is sacred:

Among these hieroglyphs, the most prominent is an altar, because among all people the civil world began with religion.   NS, 8

All nations, barbarous as well as civilized, keep these three customs: all have some religion, all contract solemn marriages, all bury their dead.   NS, 333

These are the divine institutions among the gentiles, from which came later all their human institutions.   NS, 10

Sullemn fulminance, sollemn nuptialism, sallemn sepulture and providential divining.   FW, 599

The occult tradition is an aristocratic tradition:

> *In all nations of the world the priests kept such doctrine secret even from their own plebs, whence indeed it was everywhere called secret doctrine, for sacred is as much as to say secret.* NS, 95

> *Heroic commonwealths are commonwealths of the few: the few who are beloved of Jove; the few who are sons of Jove; heroes who considered themselves sons of the gods, of whom Hercules was believed to be the greatest.* NS, 490, 53

Civilization is in origin and nature a class-structure, and history is the history of class-struggle.

The origin of cities:

> *They will be seen to be founded by nature on two communities, one of the nobles, to command, the other of the plebs, to obey.* NS, 25

Process is profanation, secularization.

In the heroic class-struggle the plebeians denied the aristocratic religion:

> *To the patricians who said in the heroic contests that the auspices were theirs, the plebs replied that the fathers of whom Romulus had composed the senate, and from whom the patricians traced their descent,* NON ESSE CAELO DEMISSOS, *"were not descended from heaven; that is, that Jove was equal to all."* NS, 508, 415

As in Fustel de Coulanges, The Ancient City.

Class-structure is rooted in religion, Vico's aristocracy is theocratic. The heroes are:

> *god-fearing giants, as opposed to the impious giants who had continued the infamous communism of things and of women.*   NS, 503 / NS, 553

> *These were at first impious men, who recognized no divinity; they were nefarious, since relations among them were not distinguished by marriages; and finally, not understanding society in the midst of this infamous promiscuity of things, they were all alone like wild beasts, and hence weak and lastly miserable and unhappy because they were in want of all the goods that are needed to keep life safe. Fleeing the several ills they suffered in the dissensions which this wild promiscuity produced, and seeking escape and safety, they betook themselves to the cultivated lands of the pious, chaste, strong, that is, of those who were already united in family society.*   NS, 17

> *To these altars, then, the impious-nomadic-weak, fleeing for their lives from the stronger, came seeking refuge, and the pious-strong killed the violent among them and took the weak under their protection.*   NS, 18

> *Grotius' simpletons and Pufendorf's abandoned men had recourse to the altars of the strong to save themselves from Hobbes' violent men.*   NS, 553

Brooding in background is the dark thought that the classes who combine to make a city are essentially heterogeneous:

The first comers to human society were driven thereto by religion and by a natural instinct to propagate the human race (the former a pious motive, the latter in the strict sense a gentle or gentile one), and thus gave a beginning to noble and lordly friendship. The second comers, since they came out of a necessity of saving their lives, gave a beginning to society in the proper sense, with a view principally to utility, and consequently base and servile. These refugees were received by the heroes under the just law of protection, by which they sustained their natural lives under the obligation of serving the heroes as day laborers.

NS, 555

Compare the primordial confrontation between Master and Slave in Hegel.

Classes are races; religion is racism:

> *The heroes or nobles, by a certain nature of theirs which they believed to be of divine origin, were led to say that the gods belonged to them, and consequently that the auspices of the gods were theirs also. By means of the auspices they kept within their own orders all the public and private institutions of the heroic cities. To the plebeians, whom they believed to be of bestial origin and consequently men without gods and hence without auspices, they conceded only the uses of natural liberty.*   NS, 414

Civilization is an altar, on which a sacrifice is being made.
Human sacrifice:

> *These sacrifices began among the first crude savage men with vows and offerings of human sacrifices.*   NS, 191, 517

Civilization is an altar:

> *Cities are called* ARAE, *altars;*   NS, 17

and arae, altars, are arable:

> *ploughed lands were the first altars of the gentiles.*   NS, 15

> *On these first lands Vesta sacrificed to Jove the impious practicers of the infamous promiscuity, who violated the first altars (the first fields of grain).*   NS, 549, 776

Vico anticipates de Maistre.

The cycle ends in a ricorso
                    recirculation   FW, 3
       Teems of times and happy returns. The seim
anew. Ordovico or viricordo.   FW, 215
Array! Surrection!   FW, 593
       The world's great age begins anew
       The golden years return
magnus ab integro saeclorum nascitur ordo
       APOTHEOSIS OF THE LUSTRAL
PRINCIPIUM   FW, 286
Revolution:
       It is just, it is just about to, it is just about to
rolywholyover.   FW, 597
A return to the first beginning
the return of the gods
the Second Coming.

       But if the peoples are rotting in that ultimate
civil disease and cannot agree on a monarch from
within, and are not conquered and preserved by
better nations from without, then providence for
their extreme ill has its extreme remedy at hand.
For such peoples, like so many beasts, have fallen
into the custom of each man thinking only of his
own private interests and have reached the extreme
of delicacy, or better of pride, in which like wild
animals they bristle and lash out at the slightest
displeasure. Thus no matter how great the throng
and press of their bodies, they live like wild beasts

in a deep solitude of spirit and will, scarcely any two being able to agree since each follows his own pleasure or caprice. By reason of all this, providence decrees that, through obstinate factions and desperate civil wars, they shall turn their cities into forests and the forests into dens and lairs of men. In this way, through long centuries of barbarism, rust will consume the misbegotten subtleties of malicious wits that have turned them into beasts made more inhuman by the barbarism of reflection than the first men had been made by the barbarism of sense. For the latter displayed a generous savagery, against which one could defend oneself or take flight or be on one's guard; but the former, with a base savagery, under soft words and embraces, plots against the life and fortune of friends and intimates. Hence peoples who have reached this point of premeditated malice, when they receive this last remedy of providence and are thereby stunned and brutalized, are sensible no longer of comforts, delicacies, pleasures, and pomp, but only of the sheer necessities of life. And the few survivors in the midst of an abundance of the things necessary for life naturally become sociable and, returning to the primitive simplicity of the first world of peoples, are again religious, truthful, and faithful. Thus providence brings back among them the piety, faith, and truth which are the natural foundations of justice as well as the graces and beauties of the eternal order of God.   NS, 1106

In the jungle of cities, the new barbarism.
It is later than you think.

> Fieluhr? Filou! What age is at? It saon is late.   FW, 213
>
> What era's o'ering? Lang gong late.   FW, 244
>
> Faurore! Fearhoure! At last it past!   FW, 587

The thing that we dread has already happened.
The thunder of the crash:

> Have you here? (Some ha) Have we where?
> (Some hant) Have you hered? (Others do) Have we
> whered? (Others dont) It's cumming, it's brumming!
> The clip, the clop! (All cla) Glass crash. The (klik-
> kaklakkaklaskaklopatzklatschabattacreppycrotty-
> graddaghsemmihsammihnouithappluddyappladdyp-
> konpkot!).   FW, 44

The sense of an ending:
Western Civilization is over.

> And the lamp went out as it couldn't glow on
> burning, yep, the lmp wnt out for it couldn't stay
> alight.   FW, 427
>
> On the verge of closing time.   FW, 474
>
> Thatll beall for tody. Cal it off. Godnotch, vry-
> boily. End a muddy crushmess!   FW, 533–34
>
> Shut up shop, dappy. And the duppy shot the
> shutter clup (Perkodhuskurunbarggruauyagokgorlay-
> orgromgremmitghundhurthrumathunaradidillifaiti-
> tillibumullunukkunun!) And they all drank free.   FW, 23

III. An Interlude of Farce

In the meantime, waiting
waiting
 Abide Zeit's sumonserving, rise afterfall.   FW, 78
Waiting for the return of the theocratic age
to greet the return of the gods
       (Heidegger
       (H.D. *Tribute to Freud*
 The while we, we are waiting, we are waiting
for. Hymn.   FW, 609

Plato:
 There is an era in which the god himself assists
the universe on its way and helps it in its rotation.
There is also an era in which he releases his control.
Thereupon it begins to revolve in a contrary direction under its own impulse. At last, as this cosmic
era draws to its close, disorder comes to a head. The
few good things the universe produces are polluted
with so great a taint of evil that it hovers on the very
brink of destruction, both it and the creatures in it.
Therefore at that very moment the god who first
set it in order looks down upon it again. Beholding
it in trouble, and anxious lest racked by storms and
confusion it suffer dissolution and sink into the
bottomless abyss of differentiation, he takes control   *Politicus,*
of the helm once more.   269c, 273d

In the meantime, an interim
in the time of the Not yet.   FW, 3
*In Nowhere has yet the Whole World taken part of
      himself for his Wife;*
*By Nowhere have Poorparents been sentenced to
      Worms, Blood and Thunder for Life*
*Not yet has the Emp from Corpsica forced the
      Arth out of Engleterre;*
*Not yet have the Sachsen and Judder on the
      Mound of a Word made Warre;*
*Not yet Witchywitchy of Wench struck Fire of his
      Heath from on Hoath;*
*Not yet his Arcobaleine forespoken Peacepeace
      upon Oath;*   FW, 175

In the interim, an interlude
      during this swishingsight teilweisioned   FW, 345
an interlude of farce.
Finnegans Wake is his farced epistol to the hibruws.   FW, 228

Etymology of farce: stuffing.
Make a farce with livers minced small. Pigge farced
with sage. With what stuffe our old historiographers
have farced up their huge volumes.   O.E.D.
Farce, or satire:
Satire. Scaliger's derivation of this word from satyr
is untenable. It is from satura (full of variety, satu-   Brewer's
rated), satura lanx, a hotchpotch or olla podrida.   Dictionary

Finnegans Wake:

My wud! The warped flooring of the lair and soundconducting walls thereof, to say nothing of the uprights and imposts, were persianly literatured with burst loveletters, telltale stories, stickyback snaps, doubtful eggshells, bouchers, flints, borers, puffers, amygdaloid almonds, rindless raisins, alphybetty- formed verbage, vivlical viasses, ompiter dictas, visus umbique, ahems and ahahs, imeffible tries at speech unasyllabled, you owe mes, eyoldhyms, fluefoul smut, fallen lucifers, vestas which had served, showered ornaments, borrowed brogues, reversibles jackets, blackeye lenses, family jars, falsehair shirts, God- forsaken scapulars, neverworn breeches, cutthroat ties, counterfeit franks, best intentions, curried notes, upset latten tintacks, unused mill and stumpling stones, twisted quills, painful digests, magnifying wineglasses, solid objects cast at goblins, once cur- rent puns, quashed quotatoes, messes of mottage, unquestionable issue papers, seedy ejaculations, limer- ick damns, crocodile tears, spilt ink, blasphematory spits, stale shestnuts, schoolgirls', young ladies', milkmaids', washerwomen's, shopkeepers' wives, merry widows', ex nuns', vice abbess's, pro virgins', super whores', silent sisters', Charleys' aunts', grand- mothers', mothers'-in-laws', fostermothers', god- mothers' garters,

A farce, or compost heap:

> *He dumptied the wholeborrow of rubbages on
> to soil here.* FW, 17

> *Puffedly offal tosh!* FW, 419

> *What a mnice old mness it all mnakes! A mid-
> denhide hoard of objects!* FW, 19

An interlude of farce
an interval

> *between shift and shift* FW, 293

> *between explosion and reexplosion (Donnaur-
> watteur! Hunderthunder!)* FW, 78

The Ginnungagap: the name given in the Icelandic
Eddas to the interval of timeless formlessness between world aeons.

> *Somewhere, parently, in the ginnandgo gap be-
> tween antediluvious and annadominant.* FW, 14

An interval of timeless formlessness
an interregnum:

Whenever the Roman constitution fell tempo-
rarily in abeyance because the succession of supreme
magistrates was accidentally broken, the transitional
period was designated an interregnum.

An interval intercalated:

An intercalary period stands outside the regular
order of things. Intercalary days tend to degenerate
into seasons of unbridled license; they form an interregnum during which customary restraints of law
and morality are suspended. Frazer,
G.B. IX, 328

Interregnum, or Saturnalia
satire for the Saturnalia.

Interlude interpolated.

Definition of farce: The word was originally applied to phrases interpolated in the litany between the words *kyrie* and *eleison*; to similar expansions of other liturgical formulae; to passages in the vernacular inserted between the Latin sentences in chanting the epistle.

O.E.D.

    His farced epistol.

FW, 228

Subsequently the name for the interludes of impromptu buffoonery which the actors in the religious dramas were accustomed to interpolate in their text.

Bob Dylan:
>   There must be some way out of here
>   Said the joker to the priest.

F. M.
Cornford

The Origin of Attic Comedy:

not the *eirōn* or the *alazōn* but the *bōmolochos*

                altar-ambusher or altar-snatcher

    James Joyce, altar-boy turned altar-snatcher.

This is the way that Shem built:

—*The hoax that joke bilked.*

—*The jest of junk the jungular?*

—*Jacked up in a jock the wrapper.*

FW, 511

Joyce celebrates the Feast of Fools
  Tis jest jibberweek's joke.   FW, 565

The festival of the subdeacons which is held on
the Circumcision or on Epiphany or the Octave of
the Epiphany is called the Feast of Fools. ('*Festum
hypodiaconorum, quod vocamus stultorum.*') This
festival flourished chiefly in the cathedral towns of
France, though there are traces of it in other coun-
tries. It varied, of course, at different places and
times, but the general character of the rejoicing is
perfectly clear, for it took the form of a complete
reversal of ordinary custom. The transformation began with the singing of the Magnificat at Vespers,
when the words 'He hath put down the mighty from
their seat and hath exalted the humble and meek'
were repeated again and again, while the *baculus* or
staff of office was delivered into the hands of one of
the despised sub-deacons who as 'bishop or Pope or
King of Fools' led his fellows into the stalls of the
higher clergy, to remain there and usurp their func-
tions for the duration of the feast. This transference
of authority was the signal for the beginning of the
most astonishing revels. As soon as the higher clergy
shed their authority the ecclesiastical ritual lost its
sanctity. Even the Mass was burlesqued. Censing
was done with pudding and sausages. Sometimes an

ass was introduced into church, while the Prose of
the Ass was chanted:

> 'Orientis partibus
> Adventavit Asinus,
> Pulcher et fortissimus,
> Sarcinis aptissimus.'

On these occasions solemn Mass was punctu-
ated with brays and howls, and the rubrics of the
'office' direct that the celebrant instead of saying
Ite missa est shall bray three times (*ter hinhannabit*)
and that the people shall respond in similar fashion.

E. Welsford,
The Fool,
202

Ritual clowns in primitive religion
the "Fools Lodge," or "Society of Contraries,"
violate taboos and thereby acquire magical power.
"You shall regard nothing as sacred."
Shocking stunts, just like Shem:

L. Makarius
in *Diogenes*,
69 (1970),
44–73

> *this mental and moral defective*

FW, 177

> *seeker of the nest of evil in the bosom of a good*
word.

FW, 189

The Zuni clowns used to drink bowls full of urine
and feed on excrement and all sorts of filthy matter.
Shem wrote *crap in his hand, sorry!*

> *He shall produce nichthemerically from his un-*
> *heavenly body a no uncertain quantity of obscene*
> *matter not protected by copriright in the United*
> *Stars of Ourania.*

FW, 185

> *This was a stinksome inkenstink*

> *The worst, it is hoped, even in our western*
> *playboyish world for pure mousefarm filth.*

FW, 183

The Zuni clowns ridicule people

Shem scrabbled and scratched and scriobbled and skrevened nameless shamelessness about everybody ever he met.

FW, 182

Other traits characteristic of ritual clowns are "reverse behaviour" and "backward speech." From his birth, the mythical Koshari, father of the Sia clowns, "talked nonsense, talked backward." The Zuni clowns say the opposite of what they mean. Like a crazy fellow. Speaking a strange language. As in *Finnegans Wake.*

It is what Michelet called "the great satanical principle that everything must be done in the reverse order."

Kish is for anticheirst, and the free of my hand to him!

FW, 308

This interlude of farce
the time of *Finnegans Wake* is intermission time
>   *incipit intermissio*   FW, 278
>   not *incipit tragoedia.*

There's just that Shakespeare fellow left to beat, said
Nora Joyce

> *He was avoopf (parn me!) aware of no other*
> *shaggspick, other Shakhisbeard, either prexactly un-*
> *like his polar andthisishis or procisely the seem as*
> *woops (parn!) as what he fancied or guessed the*
> *sames as he was himself.*   FW, 177

Joyce's answer to Shakespearian tragedy:
>   *incipit intermissio*
> *Lights, pageboy, lights!*   FW, 245

The moment of *Finnegans Wake* corresponds to the
exit of the king from the play within the play in
Hamlet:

> *Enterruption. Check or slowback. Dvershen.*   FW, 332
> *You're well held now, Missy Cheekspeer, and*
> *your panto's off!*   FW, 257

Farce makes a farce out of tragedy.

> *Have you evew thought, wepowtew,*
> *that sheew gweatness was his twadgedy?*   FW, 61

Empson, *Some Versions of Pastoral*, p. 5: "There was a performance of *Hamlet* in the Turk-Sib region which the audience decided spontaneously was farce."

Karl Marx, *The Eighteenth Brumaire of Louis Bonaparte*, p. 1: "Hegel says somewhere that, upon the stage of universal history, all great events and personalities reappear in one fashion or another. He forgot to add that on the first occasion, they appear as tragedy; on the second, as farce."

Tragedy, comedy, farce
the forms of politics are the forms of theater
bourgeois comedy, the happy ending   H. Rosenberg
tragic confrontation of antagonists
                   the agony
Class-struggle as the continuation of tragedy
Waiting for Lefty—
Is the proletariat the new collective hero
          waiting to go on stage
          another actor on the stage of history
          a new actor in a neo-classical revival
          as in 1848—
          Karl Marx of *The Communist Mani-*
          festo—
Or is the proletariat the sober reality of the human
condition
—the necessity of labor—
to be disclosed after the show is over
after the farce has ended
    *and none so soon either shall the pharce for the
nunce come to a setdown secular phoenish.*   FW, 4
Waiting for Lefty, Waiting for Godot
waiting to stop the show, the farce
waiting to bring the house down.

> *History is a nightmare from which I am trying to awake.*   Ulysses, 34

> *The play thou schouwburgst, Game, here endeth. The curtain drops by deep request.*   FW, 257

> *Roll away the reel world, the reel world, the reel world!* CHERCHONS LA FLAMME!   FW, 64

Farce is the mode of consciousness in which a people take leave of their history
"The iron statue of Napoleon will crash from the top of the Vendôme column."   Marx
No more Greek revival
let the dead bury the dead
no more ghosts.
Waiting for a new dawn.

> *Calling all downs. Calling all downs to dayne. Array! Surrection!*   FW, 593

> *You mean to see we have been hadding a sound night's sleep? You may so. It is just, it is just about to, it is just about to rolywholyover.*   FW, 597

The necessity of farce:
it takes a farce to see a farce
Marx's paradoxes in *The Eighteenth Brumaire*
it is not sober political analysis: it's a riot.
Marx clowning
Abbie Hoffman clowning
John Cage clowning
What Karl Marx really meant is *Finnegans Wake*.
"Literary bolshevism," brother Stanislaus Joyce
called it.

> *Stannie was a santryman and drilled all decent
> people. Caddy went to Winehouse and wrote o
> peace a farce.*   FW, 14

Farce, or operetta—
>   the swan song of dying civilizations—
>   *For a burning would is come to dance inane.*   FW, 250

>   *Are you not danzzling on the age of a vulcano?*
>   *Siar, I am deed.*   FW, 89

Operetta—
"Its divine idiocy, its heavenly sclerosis," to quote
the Polish novelist Witold Gombrowicz, "provide a
perfect artistic symbol for the absurdity of outworn
conventions, for paralyzed social and political struc-
tures."   *New York Times*, March 9, 1970

Finnegans Wake is Joyce's gaiety pantheomime   FW, 180
>   *or chrisman's pandemon*   FW, 455

>   *Every evening at lighting up o'clock sharp and*
>   *until further notice in Feenichts Playhouse. (Bar*
>   *and conveniences always open, Diddlem Club doun-*
>   *cestears.)*   FW, 219

>   *With futurist onehorse balletbattle pictures and*
>   *the Pageant of Past History worked up with animal*
>   *variations amid everglaning mangrovemazes and*
>   *beorbtracktors by Messrs Thud and Blunder. Shad-*
>   *ows by the film folk, masses by the good people.*   FW, 221

>   *The gist of the pantomime, from cannibal king*
>   *to the property horse, being, slumply and slopely, to*
>   *remind us how, in this drury world of ours, Father*
>   *Times and Mother Spacies boil their kettle with*
>   *their crutch. Which every lad and lass in the lane*
>   *knows. Hence.*   FW, 599–600

Farce is the mode of demystification
the tragic mode remystifies
       "Love Remystified"
the tragic mode is solempne.
The necessity of farce or *Finnegans Wake*
in order to have our archetypes without Jungian
solemnity or Yeatsian occultism.
    —*How culious an epiphany!*   FW, 508

Farce is vulgarization
    (*Stoop*)   FW, 18
       (*please stoop*)
                                   W. C.
"It is imperative that we sink"   Williams
    HYPOTHESES OF COMMONEST
    EXPERIENCES   FW, 286
Here Comes Everybody.
No more heroics
instead of Aristotle's leading families, *our low hero*   FW, 184
    O! the lowness of him was beneath all up to
that sunk to!   FW, 171
    Lowest basemeant in hystry!   FW, 535

Farce is the theater of impotence.
In a situation of general social paralysis
stasis, sterility, stereotypification
the aim is not the seizure of power, but the dissolution of power.
Karl Marx in *The Eighteenth Brumaire*
demolishing the cult of the leader
bringing Napoleon's statue down.
Abbie Hoffman: "We are outlaws, not organizers."
Organizers are big pricks.
Beyond history, beyond tragedy, beyond genital organization of the body politic.
Farce is the theater of impotence
the clown is the castrated penis   Fenichel
the little fellow; Charlie Chaplin.

Farce is nihilism.
> *Nixnixundnix.*   FW, 415
Joyce wore his eyes out looking at Europe and seeing nothing.
And of Irish history he said: Two bloody Irishmen in a bloody fight over bloody nothing.
Finnegans Wake: *Putting Allspace in a Notshall.*   FW, 455
> *All marryvoising moodmoulded cyclewheeling history.*   FW, 186

Avoiding Jungian solemnity or Yeatsian occultism
we take refuge in the Void, the Nothing:

> *It was allso agreeable in our sinegear clutch-*
> *less, touring the no placelike no timelike absolent,*
> *mixing up pettyvaughan populose with the magnu-*
> *moore genstries, lloydhaired mersscenary blookers*
> *with boydskinned pigttetails and goochlipped*
> *gwendolenes with duffyeyed dolores; like so many*
> *unprobables in their poor suit of the improssable.*   FW, 609

A tale
Told by an idiot, full of sound and fury,
Signifying nothing.   *Macbeth*, V, v

King Lear is also *Much Ado About Nothing*

Tomfoolery

Enter Lear, with Cordelia dead in his arms

My poor fool is hang'd!   *Lear*, V, iii

Beyond tragedy and farce
is the fusion of these opposites.
The final pages of *Finnegans Wake*
literature at the breaking point
breaking down
breaking into tears.

> *The poignt of fun where I am crying to arrive*
> *you at.*   FW, 160

This intermingling of hilarity and fear is, ethnologically speaking, sufficient to betray the presence of the clown.

Just as in the romantic theory of the *mélange des genres* in literature, the Zuni clowns represent both gravity and hilarity.

Makarius

In *Finnegans Wake*, the twins Hilary and Tristopher Giordano Bruno's motto: *In hilaritate tristis, in tristitia hilaris.*

I am not leering, I pink you pardons. I am highly sheshe sherious.

FW, 570

Beyond tragedy and farce
to the fusion of these opposites
is
back
back to the original goat-song out of which both
tragedy and satyr-play, those *siamixed* twins,   FW, 66
by separation arose.

      We know nothing and can know nothing
                            but
      the dance, to dance to a measure
      contrapuntally,
                 Satyrically, the tragic foot.   W. C.
                                     Williams

Tragoedia = goat-song
    What then agentlike brought about that tra-
goady thundersday this municipal sin business?   FW, 5
        This municipal sin business—is he talk-
        ing about Kent State?
    That tragoady thundersday
Finnegans Wake is *that fishabed ghoatstory*   FW, 51
HCE is *Hircus Civis Eblanensis,* old goat-citizen   FW, 215
                    of Dublin
Giles Goat-Boy is out of *Finnegans Wake*   John Barth
    Got by the one goat, suckled by the same nanna,
one twitch, one nature makes us oldworld kin.   FW, 463

Goat-song or satyr-play
satyr-play or satire
Scaliger's derivation of this word from satyr is rein-
stated when we go joycing

> > > > *letting punplays pass to ernest.*   FW, 233

> *That tragoady thundersday*
or *Satyr's Caudledayed Nice.*   FW, 415

> *For the triduum of Saturnalia his goatservant*
had paraded hiz willingsons in the Forum.   FW, 97

> *Saturnights pomps, exhabiting that corricatore*
of a harss, revealled by Oscur Camerad.   FW, 602

Finnegan Beginnagain
we are back again
before the Birth of Tragedy
before the Gods of Greece
something more elemental.

What does that synthesis of god and goat in the
satyr mean? (Nietzsche). I estimate the value of   *Ecce Homo,*
human beings, or races, according to how necessarily   XV, 4; II, 4
they cannot understand the god apart from the
satyr.
Said the joker to the priest.
Mais regardez donc ce Joyce: il est tout à fait grecque.
C'est le satyre sur un vase grecque!   Ellmann, 612

Something more elemental
the hour of the beast—*"pawses"* FW, 221

 *It darkles, (tinct, tint) all this our funnaminal
world.* FW, 244

Not Pater noster but *Panther monster.* FW, 244
Pan-ther: all beast.
When the leopards break into the temple and drink
the wine from the sacred chalice.

The hour of the beast, or the barbarian

 *The wild main from Borneholm has jest come
to crown.* FW, 331

 *The whool of the whaal in the wheel of the
whorl of the Boubou from Bourneum has thus come
to taon!* FW, 415

 *One two three. Chours! So come on, ye wealthy
gentrymen wibfrufrocksfull of fun! Thin thin! Thin
thin! Thej olly and thel ively, thou billy with thee
coo, for to jog a jig of a crispness nice and sing a
missal too. Hip champouree! Hiphip champouree!
O you longtailed blackman, polk it up behind me!
Hip champouree! Hiphip champouree! And, jessies,
push the pumkik round. Anneliuia!* FW, 236

 *One stands, given a grain of goodwill, a fair
chance of actually seeing the whirling dervish, Tu-
mult, son of Thunder.* FW, 184

Waiting for the return of the gods
witnessing the return of barbarism
                              the new barbarians
Engels, on *The Origin of the Family, Private Property
                              and the State*:
the origin—the coming-into-being and the passing-
away—
"Indeed, only barbarians are capable of rejuvenating
a world laboring under the death throes of unnerved
civilization."
Vico is right
Engels is right—

         Here is that synthesis that Gramsci sought:
         Vico and Marxism reconciled—
Mao is right—

         The Great Cultural Revolution was to de-
tach communism from civilization. The civilized
world looked on and could not believe its eyes.

Waiting for the return of the gods
witnessing the return of barbarism
The new barbarians
    *returning to primitive simplicity of the first
world of peoples*   NS, 1106
to recognize the gods
to greet them
Dei dialectus soloecismus—the dialect of God is   *Love's Body,*
                                 solecism.   *239*
God does not speak good English.
Not atticism but solecism.
Barbarism.

Barbarism, or speaking with tongues
               as in *Finnegans Wake*
                   polyglot turning into glossolalia
Pentecost
    *wordloosed over seven seas crowdblast in cellel-
leneteutoslavzendlatinsoundscript.*   FW, 219
    *In the buginning is the woid, in the muddle is
the sounddance.*   FW, 378
Instead of the sentence, the sounddance.

IV. The New Science of Origins

Vico is *ricorso*

The *New Science* is return to divination:

> *This Science must therefore be a rational civil theology of divine providence.*   NS, 342

> "Though created in the second-cycle age of men, its creation has been made possible by a return to the poetic wisdom by which the world of nations was first created."   NS, K7

A return to the language of the gods:

> *Their poetic wisdom began with this poetic metaphysics, which contemplated God by the attribute of his providence; and they were called theological poets, or sages who understood the language of the gods expressed in the auspices of Jove; and were properly called divine in the sense of diviners, from* DIVINARI, *to divine or predict.*   NS, 381

The gods return in thunder:
> Reader! lover of books! lover of heaven,
> And of that God from whom all things are given,
> Who in mysterious Sinai's awful cave
> To Man the wondrous art of writing gave:
> Again he speaks in thunder and in fire!
> Thunder of Thought, and flames of fierce desire:

Blake,
Jerusalem,
pl. 3

The gods return in thunder
Finnegans Wake is thunder
Vico is thunder; stunning
Vico's best reader, Michelet:

"1824. Vico. Effort, infernal shades, grandeur, the golden bough. From 1824 on, I was seized by a frenzy caught from Vico, an incredible intoxication with his great historical principle."

Autob. 76

The origin of civilization, thunder:

For a long period of time the impious races of the children of Noah, having lapsed into a state of bestiality, went wandering like wild beasts until they were scattered and dispersed through the great forest of the earth; and with their bestial education giants had sprung up and existed among them at the time when the heavens thundered for the first time after the flood.   NS, 195

Thereupon a few giants, who must have been the most robust, and who were dispersed through the forests on the mountain heights where the strongest beasts have their dens, were frightened and astonished by the great effect whose cause they did not know, and raised their eyes and became aware of the sky. They pictured the sky to themselves as a great animated body, which in that aspect they called Jove, the first god of the so-called greater gentes, who meant to tell them something by the hiss of his bolts and the clap of his thunder.   NS, 377

Thus it was fear which created gods in the world.   NS, 382

God-fearing giants, as represented by the Polyphemus of Homer.   NS, 503

For the Clearer of the Air from on high has spoken in tumbuldum tambaldam to his tembledim tombaldoom worrild and, moguphonoised by that phonemanon, the unhappitents of the earth have terrerumbled from fimament unto fundament and from tweedledeedumms down to twiddledeedees.   FW, 258

What the thunder said
DA DA DA
Damyata: Restrain yourselves
That frightful thought of some divinity which imposed form and measure on the bestial passions of these lost men and thus transformed them into human passions.   NS, 340

The giants, enchained under the mountains by the frightful religion of the thunderbolts, learned to check their bestial habit of wandering wild through the great forest of the earth, and acquired the contrary custom of remaining hidden and settled in their fields. With this conatus the virtue of spirit began likewise to show itself among them, restraining also their bestial lust from finding its satisfaction in the sight of heaven, of which they had a mortal terror. So it came about that each of them would drag one woman into his cave and would keep her there in perpetual company for the duration of their lives. Thus the act of human love was performed under cover, in hiding, that is to say, in shame; and this, after religion, is the second bond that keeps nations united, even as shamelessness and impiety destroy them.   NS, 504

The origin of civilization, thunder; the origin of
civilization, madness
Hexagram 16. Yü/Enthusiasm

　　— —
　　— —
　　————
　　— —
　　— —
　　— —

"Thunder comes resounding out of the earth: the
image of enthusiasm."

*It was a deficiency of human reasoning power
that gave rise to poetry so sublime that the philos-
ophies which came afterward have produced none
equal or better, and have even prevented its pro-
duction.*   NS, 384

Vico recovers that heroic sublimity
his ΦBK speech to the students in 1732:
della mente eroica.
Writing *The New Science*
>   *this work has filled me with a certain heroic
spirit.*   Autob. 15
>>   *Lightning-like flashes of Platonic divinity.*   Autob. 138
>>   *Cultivating a kind of divinity in our mind.*   Autob. 141

Vico recovers that creative madness, or fury:
>   *An almost fatal fury drove him to meditate it
and write it so rapidly, indeed, that he began it
Christmas morning 1729 and finished it at nine
o'clock Easter Sunday evening (April 9, 1730).*   Autob. 194
Fatal fury, heroic fury
Eroici Furori, Giordano Bruno; who got terribly
burned
another Orphic voice, another Neo-Platonist.
Vico belongs to the Hermetic tradition.

The origin of language in fantasy, not in reality:
>   *For that first language, spoken by the theologi-
cal poets, was not a language in accord with the nature of the things it dealt with, but was a fantastic
speech making use of physical substances endowed
with life and most of them imagined to be divine.*   NS, 401

Hence poetic wisdom, the first wisdom of the gentile world, must have begun with a metaphysics not rational and abstract like that of learned men now, but felt and imagined as that of these first men must have been who, without power of ratiocination, were all robust sense and vigorous imagination.

NS, 375

It is beyond our power to enter into the vast imagination of these first men, whose minds were not in the least abstract, refined or spiritualized, because they were entirely immersed in the senses, buffeted by passions, buried in the body.

NS, 378

They were out of their minds:

For God, in his purest intelligence, knows things, and, by knowing them, creates them; but they, in their robust ignorance, did it by virtue of a wholly corporeal imagination. And because it was quite corporeal, they did it with marvellous sublimity; a sublimity such and so great that it excessively perturbed the very persons who by imagining did the creating, for which they were called poets, which is Greek for "creators."

NS, 376

That such was the origin of poetry is finally confirmed by this eternal property of it: that its proper material is the credible impossibility.

NS, 383

Man is maniac
the Dionysian origin of civilization
enthusiasm

So that, as rational metaphysics teaches that man becomes all things by understanding them (HOMO INTELLIGENDO FIT OMNIA), *this imaginative metaphysics shows that man becomes all things by not understanding them* (HOMO NON INTELLIGENDO FIT OMNIA).

NS, 405

It's all a misunderstanding, a creative misunderstanding
the fortunate fall

Hirp! Hirp! for their Missed Understandings! chirps the Ballat of Perce-Oreille.

FW, 175

Myths arising from art forms misunderstood, arising from facts misunderstood, arising from historical events, arising from literary allusions misunderstood, arising from metaphor, giving rise to would-be history.

R. Duncan,
*Truth & Life
of Myth,* 47

The original mistake in every sentence: metaphor.

Love's Body,
244

Vico is ricorso
Vico a poet-giant
wandering in the primeval forest again:

> *We wander ignorant of the men and the places.* Autob. 49

> *You is feeling like you was lost in the bush,*
boy? You says: It is a puling sample jungle of woods. FW, 112
The rediscovery of the uncertainty principle
in Heisenberg, in Joyce, in John Cage.

> *along the winding ways of random ever!* FW, 405

> *(since in this scherzarade of one's thousand*
one nightinesses that sword of certainty which would
indentifide the body never falls) FW, 51

> *in fact, the sameold gamebold adomic structure*
of our Finnius the old One, as highly charged with
electrons as hophazards can effective it. FW, 615

Vico rebarbarizing himself

    To discover the way in which the first human thinking arose in the gentile world, we encountered exasperating difficulties which have cost us the research of a good twenty years. We had to descend from these human and refined natures of ours to those quite wild and savage natures, which we cannot at all imagine and can comprehend only with great efforts.

NS, 338

It is a learned ignorance, as in Cusanus

Nicholas of Cusa: another Orphic voice.

The solution to the problem of identity: Get lost.

Love's Body, 161

    We are once amore as babes awqndering in a wold made fresh where with the hen in the story-aboot we start from scratch.

FW, 336

    The woods are fond always. As were we their babes in. And robins in crews so.

FW, 619

V. The New Science of Language

Man is his own maker
maker or creator
creator or poet
    "Poets," which is Greek for "creators."   NS, 376

The making is poetry, poiesis   Hölderlin,
Dichterisch wohnet der Mensch auf dieser Erde   Heidegger
there is only poetry   *Love's Body,*
the key to The New Science is poetry: 266

    *The principle of these origins both of languages
and of letters lies in the fact that the first gentile
peoples, by a demonstrated necessity of nature, were
poets who spoke in poetic characters. This discovery,
which is the master key of this Science, has cost us
the persistent research of almost all our literary life,
because with our civilized natures we cannot at all
imagine and can understand only by great toil the
poetic nature of these first men.*   NS, 34

Man makes himself by making his own gods, and
this is poetry.

In the Autobiography Vico summarizes:

*He discovers new historical principles of philos-
ophy, and first of all a metaphysics of the human
race. That is to say, a natural theology of all nations
by which each people naturally created by itself its
own gods through a certain natural instinct that
man has for divinity. Thus he discovers the identity
of the grand principle of gentile theology with that
of the poetry of the theological poets, who were the
world's first poets.*

Autob. 167–8

The key to The New Science is mythology
but the key to mythology is etymology:

*Meanwhile Vico, by the reading of Bacon of
Verulam's treatise* ON THE WISDOM OF THE ANCIENTS,
*more ingenious and learned than true, was incited
to look for its principles farther back than in the
fables of the poets. He was moved to do this by the
example of Plato who in the* CRATYLUS *had sought to
track them down within the origins of the Greek
language. An added incentive was the feeling he had
begun to entertain, that the etymologies of the
grammarians were unsatisfactory.*

Autob. 148

Anthropology becomes linguistics; or philosophical philology:

"A New Science is Essayed," wherein he begins to reduce philology to scientific principles.   Autob. 158

Including among the philologians all the grammarians, historians, critics, who have occupied themselves with the study of the languages and deeds of peoples.   NS, 139

Overcoming the Cartesian bias against philology:

The philosophers failed by half in not giving certainty to their reasonings by appeal to the authority of philologians, and likewise the latter failed by half in not taking care to give their authority the sanction of truth by appeal to the reasoning of the philosophers.   NS, 140

Dethroning philosophy in favor of mythology:

It follows that the first science to be learned should be mythology or the interpretation of fables.   NS, 51

Truth and life is in myth:

Poetic truth is metaphysical truth, and physical truth which is not in conformity with it should be considered false.   NS, 205

Thus he overthrows the rationalist theory of the origin of the state: a social contract based on prudential considerations that made sense to enlightended philosophers of the Age of Reason.

Hugo Grotius, John Selden, and Samuel Pufendorf should have taken their start from the beginnings of the gentes, where their subject-matter begins. But all three of them err together in this respect, by beginning in the middle; that is, with the latest times of the civilized nations (and thus of men enlightened by fully developed natural reason).

NS, 394

The foundation of the state is returned to Orpheus, who with his song tamed the savage beasts; to Amphion, who with his lyre built out of stocks and stones the walls of a city.

Amphion used stones, in the sense in which the Latin word for stone, LAPIS, *meant a lout, and signifying therefore the simple-minded plebeians.*

NS, 734

The metaphysics of the poet-giants, by making them god-fearing, was the source of their poetic morality.

NS, 502

Cosmos upsung from chaos:

through the windr of a wondr in a wildr is a weltr as a wirbl of a warbl is a world.

FW, 597

Corollary: That the Ancient Roman Law was a Serious Poem, and that the Ancient Jurisprudence a Severe Kind of Poetry.

NS, 1027

Legal Fiction is Poetic Diction:

Owen Barfield

Thus all the fictions of ancient jurisprudence were truths under masks, and the formulae in which the laws were expressed, because of their strict measures of such and so many words—admitting neither addition, subtraction, nor alteration—were called CARMINA, *or songs.*

NS, 1036

* * * * *

The New Science of language
the nature of words is their nascimento
     their origin
     their etymology.
The etymology of the word etymology:
etym means true
  the definition of the word "etymology"
itself as meaning VERILOQUIUM.

NS, 403

The truth is in the root
the true meaning is the original meaning.

Anthropology is history, and history is etymology:

This was the order of human institutions: first the forests, after that the huts, then the villages, next the cities, and finally the academies.

This axiom is a great principle of etymology, for this sequence of human institutions sets the pattern for the histories of words in the various native languages. Thus we observe in the Latin language that almost the whole corpus of its words had sylvan or rustic origins. For example, LEX. First it must have meant a collection of acorns. Thence we believe is derived ILEX, as it were ILLEX, the oak (as certainly AQUILEX means collector of waters); for the oak produces the acorns by which the swine are drawn together. LEX was next a collection of vegetables, from which the latter were called LEGUMINA. Later on, at a time when vulgar letters had not yet been invented for writing down the laws, LEX by a necessity of civil nature must have meant a collection of citizens, or the public parliament; so that the presence of the people was the LEX, or "law." Finally, collecting letters, and making, as it were, a sheaf of them for each word, was called LEGERE, reading. NS, 239–40

A *very fairworded instance of falsemeaning adamelegy.*

FW, 77

But we are

making a bolderdash for lubberty of speech letting punplays pass to ernest.

FW, 233

History is paronomastic

—*History as her is harped.*

FW, 486

The texture of history is the texture of *Finnegans Wake.*

Compare Marcel Granet, *Chinese Civilization:*

198–99

Yao, the Sovereign who "appeared like the sun" had to aim arrows at the sun before he could become a Son of Heaven. Thus he succeeded in overcoming his celestial double. As soon as he had conquered the emblem of the sun, he was worthy to reign. Archery is an inaugural ceremony by which one can reveal one's virtue. But an unworthy Chieftain will see the proof turn against him. The penalty which overtakes the incapable magician is the result of a reflex action, the arrows which are aimed at Heaven fall back in the form of lightning. The bowman himself is struck by lightning, and perishes, because without possessing the necessary qualifications, he has attempted to awaken and capture the energies of the Fire. Such was the case of Wu-yi, a king without Virtue. Wu-yi shot an arrow aiming at the sky, or rather at a leather

bottle full of blood which he called the Sky. Made
of the skin of a bull, it had the shape of an owl. The
king drew his bow after he had won *the owl's move*
at a game of chess which gave him the right to try his
fortune. Wu-yi belonged to the family of the Yin,
who owned the emblem of the Owl and bore the
name *Leather Bottle*. But, being degenerate, he had
not the virtue in himself which empowered him to
be worthy his coat-of-arms and to remain master of
his mythical double. It was quite otherwise with
Huang-ti. Huang-ti (the yellow Sovereign) was able
to catch Owls (Yellow Birds). A true sovereign ought
to be able to shoot them by using twisted arrows.
Like the lightning, these are the bearers of fire.
Huang-ti, who fed upon owls, knew how to identify
himself completely with his emblem. By means of
sacraments, all the virtue of the celestial fires was
incorporated in him. He was thus enabled to ascend
to heaven by apotheosis in a hurricane.

Huang-ti was thunder. He was also identified
with a celestial Leather Bottle, under the name of
Ti-hong. The leather bottle Ti-hong is a bird as well
as a bag made of skins and a drum. There is even an
owl (his name is Drum-of-the-Night) who is a bag,
and from whom thunderbolt and arrows will re-

bound. And finally, there is a drum who is an owl, producing the wind when he breathes. Completely red and with immovable eyes, he represents a forge and its bellows. The Celestial Leather Bottle is red also, like mineral ore in fusion, and at the summit of the Hill of Heaven, which is rich in copper. It bears the name: Chaos (*Hun-tun*). Chaos dies when it is pierced seven times by the Lightning. But this death is only a second birth. It is an initiation. As a matter of fact, every man has seven apertures in his face. But only a respectable (*i.e.*, a well-born) man has seven to his heart. Hun-tun, the Leather-bottle Chaos, when he was personified, was represented as a stupid busybody. He had no aperture: he had "neither visage, nor eyes," that is to say, he lacked *face*, or respectability. In a mythical drama in which he figures, he is born anew in the end, by means of execution. In his right as celestial Leather Bottle, he takes part in a dance, and he is shown besides offering a banquet. It is precisely to the Lightnings that he offers it, and if they pierce him seven times, it is not with evil intent and in order to kill him: they mean to pay him for his kind reception.

* * * * *

The New Science is etymology:
In the beginning was the Word, and the Word was
Man.
Man is grammar:
Tenses and Persons of the Verb
a city is syntax
            (Karl Kraus

Etymology is *ricorso*: as it was in the beginning.
As in *Finnegans Wake*:

    the abnihilisation of the etym.   FW, 353

That's what *Finnegans Wake* is about:
smashing the atom.
Etyms are atoms.
Annihilisation of language:

    *he would wipe alley english spooker, multa-
phoniaksically spuking, off the face of the erse.*   FW, 178

Annihilisation of language so that it can be abnihi-
lated again; created out of nothing.
Out of the thunder:

    *The abnihilisation of the etym by the grisning
of the grosning of the grinder of the grunder of the
first lord of Hurtreford expolodotonates through
Parsuralia with an ivanmorinthorrorumble fragorom-
boassity amidwhiches general uttermosts confussion
are perceivable moletons skaping with mulicules
while coventry plumpkins fairlygosmotherthemselves
in the Landaunelegants of Pinkadindy.*   FW, 353

Etymology: the origin of language

    A fantastic speech making use of physical substances endowed with life and most of them imagined to be divine.

NS, 401

First comes a body language:

    The universal principle of etymology in all languages: words are carried over from bodies and from the properties of bodies to signify the institutions of the mind and spirit.

NS, 237

First comes the senses:

    What Aristotle said of the individual man is therefore true of the race in general: NIHIL EST IN INTELLECTU QUIN PRIUS FUERIT IN SENSU. *That is, the human mind does not understand anything of which it has had no previous impression from the senses.*

NS, 363

But these are not the sensations of vulgar empiricism. The atoms or etyms of language, the roots, are not prosaic sensations but poetic genera.

Poetic genera, or poetic characters.

Not intelligible class concepts of things,

but imaginative class concepts:

    The first men, the children, as it were, of the human race, not being able to form intelligible class concepts of things, had a natural need to create poetic characters; that is, imaginative class concepts or universals, to which, as to certain models or ideal portraits, to reduce all the particular species which resembled them.

NS, 209

Imaginative class concepts, or mythologies:

Thus the mythologies must have been the proper languages of the fables, as their name indicates; the fables being imaginative class concepts, the mythologies must have been the allegories corresponding to them.

NS, 403

Poetic genera, or sensory topics:

The first founders of humanity applied themselves to a sensory topics by which they brought together those properties or qualities or relations of individuals and species which were, so to speak, concrete, and from these created their poetic genera.

NS, 495

"It was by a topos, or common 'place' that primitive men passed from the thundering sky to Jove the Thunderer."

NS, K7n

This is the way in which the theological poets apprehended Jove, Cybele, and Neptune, for example, and, at first mutely pointing, explained them as substances of the sky, the earth, and the sea, which they imagined to be animate divinities and were therefore true to their senses in believing them to be gods.

NS, 402

Sensory topics are:

Sensible signs believed to be divine counsels sent to man by the gods.

NS, 366

Signification is of signs and wonders.

Civilization originates in stammering

    half a sylb, helf a solb, holf a salb onward   FW, 292

The builder is a stutterer:

    Then inmaggin a stotterer. Suppoutre him to
been one biggermaster Omnibil.   FW, 337

Balbus babbles; Balbus builder of the Tower of Babel.   FW, 467

The thunder is God stuttering:

            to speak broken heaventalk   FW, 261

    The sibspeeches of all mankind have foliated
(earth seizing them!) from the root of some fun-
ner's stotter.   FW, 96

    *   *   *   *   *

    First the divine, a dumb language of hiero-
glyphics.   Autob. 169

Mute speech is hieroglyph and body speech,
stammering and poetry, highest and lowest,
seen as one.

    Now in view of the nature of children and the
custom of the first Egyptians, we assert that poetic
speech, in virtue of the poetic characters it employs,
can yield many important discoveries concerning
antiquity.   NS, 413

The original language is the language of the gods
the language of the gods is mute speech.
Myth is mute speech:

> In Greek the fable was also called MYTHOS,
> myth, whence comes Latin MUTUS, mute. For speech
> was born in mute times as a mental language, which
> Strabo in a golden passage says existed before vocal
> or articulate language.

NS, 401

> The first language, that of the times of the
> families when gentile men were newly received into
> humanity, was a mute language of signs and physical
> objects having natural relations to the ideas they
> wished to express.

NS, 32

> It must have been the most ancient language of
> Atlantis.

NS, 431

The language of the gods is not spoken words but signs:

> *They believed that Jove commanded by signs, that such signs were words, and that nature was the language of Jove.*   NS, 379

Signification is of signs and wonders.

What the thunder said

dumbfounding

> *wonderstruck us as a thunder, yunder.*   FW, 57

> *Well, all be dumbed!*   FW, 262

> *Imagine the twelve deaferended dumbbawls of whowl abovebeugled to be the contonuation through regeneration of the urutteration of the word in pregross.*   FW, 284

> *Ullhodturdenweirmudgaardgringnirurdrmolnir-fenrirlukkilokkibaugimandodrrerinsurtkrinmgern-rackinarockar! Thor's for yo!*

> *—The hundredlettered name again, last word of perfect language.*   FW, 424

Mute speech
> science of sonorous silence   FW, 230
> all's set for restart after the silence   FW, 382
> > the shocking silence   FW, 393
> The silence speaks the scene.   FW, 13

Divination of signs and wonders
> "In a Symbol there is concealment and yet reve-
> lation: here therefore, by Silence and by Speech   Love's Body,
> acting together, comes a double significance."   190
> > words of silent power   FW, 345
> Silence in thought! Spreach! Wear anartful of
> outer nocense!   FW, 378

> First the divine, a dumb language of hiero-   Autob. 169;
> glyphics or sacred characters. Poetic characters.   NS, 34

Poetry precedes prose
but poetry is writing; characters;
graven images; hieroglyphs; ideograms; Anathemata;   D. Jones
pictograms
Fenollosa, The Chinese Written Character as a
Medium for Poetry.

Imagism
language as epiphany
flashes (of lightning)
> *Where flash becomes word and silents selfloud.*   FW, 267
> 'Tis *optophone which ontophanes.*   FW, 13
>> optophone—is it optical or optimal?

It is both. Two words get on top of each other and become sexual.

The elements of language are sensory topics
sensory topics are poetic images
etyms are images
the Chinese written character is visible etymology.

> "The etymologist finds the deadest word to have been once a brilliant picture. Language is fossil poetry."   Emerson

Poetry comes before prose: that is to say writing comes before speech.

All nations began to speak by writing.   NS, 429

Or a more moderate formulation:

Philologists have believed that languages first came into being and then letters; whereas letters and language were born twins and proceeded apace through all their three stages.   NS, 33

A reproach to the whole trend of twentieth-century philosophy of language.

But a correction is coming from M. Foucault, *Les Mots et les choses*; and J. Derrida, *De la grammatologie*. (And from the decipherment of the genetic codex.)

Foucault and Derrida return to the occult tradition
the doctrine of signs as signatures of things
signification is of signatures

The Signature Of All Things   Boehme

What God deposited in the world was written words; Adam, when he first assigned names to the beasts, was reading these visible and silent marks, this mute speech.   Foucault, 53

It is all one book
The Book of God's Works and the Book of God's
Word.
Every phenomenon is scripture
not alphabetic but hieroglyphic.

   Find tongues in trees, books in the running
brooks,
      Sermons in stones, and God in every thing.
      Astrology, the science of the speech of the stars.   NS, 739
      He lifts the lifewand and the dumb speak.
      —*Quoiquoiquoiquoiquoiquoiquoiq!*   FW, 195

Everything is legend: to be read (*lego, legere,* to
read)
to be deciphered
Denise Levertov, "To The Reader"

      As you read, a white bear leisurely
      pees, dyeing the snow
      saffron,

      and as you read, many gods
      lie among lianas: eyes of obsidian
      are watching the generations of leaves,

      and as you read
      the sea is turning its dark pages,
      turning
      its dark pages.

Mute speech
"—Say it, no ideas but in things—"

W. C.
Williams

Thus the first peoples, who were the children of the human race, founded the first world upon the arts; the arts are nothing but imitations of nature, and in a certain way "real" poems made not of words but of things.

NS, 217, 498

Idanthyrsus, king of the Scythians, used five real words to answer Darius the Great. These five were a frog, a mouse, a bird, a ploughshare, and a bow.

NS, 435

Five real words
say it with things

"Rebus (Lat. with things). A hieroglyphic riddle, *non verbis sed rebus*. The origin of the word has, somewhat doubtfully, been traced to the lawyers of Paris who, during the carnival, used to satirize the follies of the day in squibs called *De rebus quae geruntur* (on the current events), and to avoid libel actions, employed hieroglyphics either wholly or in part."

Finnegans Wake.

"In heraldry the name rebus is given to punning devices on a coat of arms suggesting the name of the family to whom it belongs; as the broken spear on the shield of Nicholas Breakspear."

*Brewer's
Dictionary*

Mute speech
say it with things, say it with deeds

A *hieroglyphic or sacred or secret language, by means of mute acts.*   NS, 32

Mute speech: In the beginning was the deed, and the deed was the word.

Three kinds of languages. The first of these was a divine mental language by mute religious acts or divine ceremonies, from which there survived in Roman law the ACTUS LEGITIMI *which accompanied all their civil transactions.*   NS, 928–29

Such ceremonial gestures are proper to mute times.   NS, 1027

Hence with regard to what is just, the certain began in mute times with the body. Then when the so-called articulate languages were invented, it advanced to ideas made certain by spoken formulae.   NS, 1045

A rebus, a riddle
a puzzle which can only be solved by turning it around in every direction:

But by writing thithaways end to end and turning, turning and end to end hithaways writing and with lines of litters slittering up and louds of latters slettering down, the old semetomyplace and jupetbackagain from tham Let Rise till Hum Lit. Sleep, where in the waste is the wisdom?   FW, 114

A rebus, a riddle
Alles Vergängliche ist nur ein Gleichniss
every phenomenon is an enigma
the new science is divination
the new science is heraldry
(iconology

*By following up these principles, he discovers
new origins of heroic insignia, which were the
dumb language of all the first nations at a time
when they were incapable of articulate speech. Thus
he discovers new principles of the science of heraldry,
which he shows to be the same as those of numis-
matics.*   Autob. 168

The New Science is heraldry
to read the Shield of Achilles
with all of history on it
history a mute poem, a work of art
and every field a heraldic shield:

*The first shield in the world was the ground of
the field where the dead were buried, whence in the
science of heraldry the shield is the ground of the
arms.*   NS, 563

To rise from history to mystery:

Love's Body,
214

Thanks, beloved, to Adam, our former first Finnlatter and our grocerest churcher, as per Grippiths' varuations, for his beautiful crossmess parzel.

FW, 619

To find significance we must learn how to read the signs, the insignia

A coat of arms was called by the Italians IN-SEGNA, an ensign in the sense of a thing signifying, whence the Italian verb INSEGNARE, to teach.

NS, 486

The hieroglyphs

The civil world or world of nations has as the elements of which it is formed all the institutions represented by the hieroglyphs displayed in the picture placed as frontispiece to serve as an introduction to THE NEW SCIENCE.

NS, 2

We start from scratch

FW, 336

"Relearning the Alphabet"

(Denise Levertov

(Stoop) if you are abcdminded, to this claybook, what curios of signs (please stoop), in this allaphbed! Can you rede its world?

FW, 18

The moral is: stop talking and start writing.

Home all go. Halome. Blare no more ramsblares, oddmund barkes! And cease your fumings, kindalled bushies! And sherrigoldies yeassymgnays; your wildeshaweshowe moves swiftly sterneward! For here the holy language. Soons to come. To pausse.

FW, 256

McLuhan is not right (write)
in the beginning was the book.

 The proteiform graph itself is a polyhedron of
scripture.   FW, 107

The new barbarism
wandering in the woods again
will rediscover the book.
Druids again: Great Scott!
     Scott's tree—
wandering in the woods
in the littering leaves renewal of letters:

 The letter! The litter! And the soother the
bitther!   FW, 93

the tree alphabet (Robert Graves)
rune, futhorc, ogham:

 All the airish signics of her dipandump helpa-
bit from an Father Hogam till the Mutther Masons.   FW, 223

The spelling, the spells:

 And how they cast their spells upon, the fronds
that thereup float, the bookstaff branchings! The
druggeted stems, the leaves incut on trees! Do you
can their tantrist spellings? I can lese, skillmistress
aiding. Elm, bay, this way, cull dare, take a message,
tawny runes ilex sallow, meet me at the pine.   FW, 571

Man is "the language animal"   G. Steiner
but if language is writing
and all nature is written
then all animals are language animals.
It is as scripture that man becomes part of nature
again;
as he becomes mythy again; that is to say, mute.

*For speech was born in mute times as a mental
language. It was fitting that the matter should be
so ordered by divine providence in religious times,
for it is an eternal property of religions that they
attach more importance to meditation than to
speech.*   NS, 401

Language and Nature, words and things (*Les Mots
et les choses*) are not heterogeneous substances.
Nature is the language of Jove.   NS, 379
Vico overcomes the disastrous dualism of the seven-
teenth century, *res cogitans* and *res extensa*.
As in *Finnegans Wake*.
Finnegans Wake is not about anything, it is that
thing itself.

*   *   *   *   *

The original language is universal human
catholic
quod semper quod ubique quod ab omnibus
archetypal

   *There must be in the nature of human institu-
tions a mental language common to all nations,
which uniformly grasps the substance of things
feasible in human social life and expresses it with as
many diverse modifications as these same things
may have diverse aspects.*   NS, 161

   *This common mental language is proper to our
Science, by whose light linguistic scholars will be
enabled to construct a mental vocabulary common
to all the various articulate languages living and
dead.*   NS, 162

   *The mental dictionary by which to interpret
properly all the various articulated languages.*   NS, 35, 145, 445
A deep structure of linguistic universals
but not as in Chomsky.

   *A universal etymologicon for the science of
language is necessary if we are to be able to discuss
with propriety the natural law of the peoples.*   Autob. 168

But deeds are words
    iconology is etymology
    anthropology is etymology
                (structuralism
    A lexicon is necessary for learning the language spoken by the ideal eternal history traversed in time by the histories of all nations.   NS, 35
    A mental vocabulary of human social institutions.   NS, 355

Along these lines there is even a way to transcend Vico's occultist elitism.
The original elite were theological poets
But in a deeper view:
    We must deny to Homer any kind of esoteric wisdom.   NS, 787
    The Greek peoples were themselves Homer.   NS, 875
Poetry is popular:
    Poetic sublimity is inseparable from popularity.   NS, 809

The language belongs to the people
and the poetry is in the language.
Let IT speak, the ID
Das Buch von dem Es
In Homer, Goethe found *eine Sprache die für sich dichtet und denket:*
a language that in and by itself makes the poetry
and does the thinking.

We must therefore proceed from a vulgar metaphysics.

NS, 340

The vulgar tongues should be the most weighty witnesses concerning those ancient customs of the peoples that were in use at the time the languages were formed.

NS, 151

Vulgar traditions must have had public grounds of truth, by virtue of which they came into being and were preserved by entire peoples over long periods of time.

NS, 149, 356

There is the common sense of the human race as the criterion taught to the nations by divine providence to define what is certain in the natural law of the gentes.

NS, 142, 145

This is the Dionysian turn to the common man.

τὸ πλῆθος ὅ τι τὸ φαυλότερον
ἐνόμισε χρῆταί τε, τόδ᾽ ἂν δεχοίμαν.

The customs and beliefs of the vulgar are normative. The mass line.

Euripides,
Bacchae,
430

The vernacular, the vulgar eloquence
the Vico Rd a public way
it is the Joycean principle of HCE
Here Comes Everybody

> *The soul of everyelsesbody rolled into its ole-soleself.*   FW, 329

The way *Finnegans Wake* was written:

> "Really it is not I who am writing this crazy book. It is you, and you, and you, and that man over there, and that girl at the next table."

> *His producers are they not his consumers?*   FW, 497

It is the way towards the unification of the human race.

> *The map of the souls' groupography.*   FW, 476

VINTAGE CRITICISM,
LITERATURE, MUSIC, AND ART